T0090598

# ULTIMATE HOPE
## FOR CHANGING TIMES

8 Studies for Individuals or Groups

DALE AND SANDY LARSEN

Harold Shaw Publishers • Wheaton, Illinois

ISBN 0-87788-842-6

Cover photo © 1999 by Luci Shaw

# CONTENTS

# INTRODUCTION

"What's going to happen?"

We've all asked the question many times over in various situations. The coming of a new century and a new millennium leads us to wonder about the future with even more intensity and with a unique mix of anticipation and anxiety. Some people at this time in history are wildly optimistic; others are frightened. Still others don't care what happens to the rest of the world, so long as they personally make the most of every opportunity in the new era.

Sometimes we ask "What's going to happen?" in an abstract sense, wondering about the long-term future of human society or the planet we live on. Sometimes the question is more immediate, when we relate it to our families or friends. We may ask with compelling urgency, focused on our fear of the next few hours or even minutes.

In all these cases we want to know what our future is going to look like. And in all these cases we fail to find the concrete answers we crave. Consistently, maddeningly, the details of the future remain hidden from us.

"What's going to happen?" Only God, the All-Knowing, knows the answer fully.

So if we know God and God knows everything, shouldn't we as his children have a special hot line to the future? The truth is that God has chosen to conceal the future from us. Instead of satisfying our curiosity with detailed information, God offers something better—*hope.* Hope for each day and hope for the future. Hope does not attempt to answer "What's going to happen?" Hope asks "Who holds my life?" and trusts the One who knows the future.

Christian hope is very different from wishful thinking or sunny optimism, as in "I hope the stock market doesn't crash" or "I hope the next decade brings me health and prosperity." The hope which God offers is confidence in the certainty of who he is. His hope goes beyond the ups and downs of the world economy or our physical health. God assures us that no matter how bad or good things are now, ultimately, something far more awesome is on the way for his people!

# HOW TO USE THIS STUDYGUIDE

Fisherman studyguides are based on the inductive approach to Bible study. Inductive study is discovery study; we discover what the Bible says as we ask questions about its content and search for answers. This is quite different from the process in which a teacher *tells* a group *about* the Bible, what it means, and what to do about it. In inductive study God speaks directly to each of us through his Word.

A group functions best when a leader keeps the discussion on target, but this leader is neither the teacher nor the "answer person." A leader's responsibility is to *ask*—not *tell*. The answers come from the text itself as group members examine, discuss, and think together about the passage.

There are four kinds of questions in each study. The first is an *approach question*. Used before the Bible passage is read, this question breaks the ice and helps you focus on the topic of the Bible study. It begins to reveal where thoughts and feelings need to be transformed by Scripture.

Some of the earlier questions in each study are *observation questions* designed to help you find out basic facts—who, what, where, when, and how.

When you know what the Bible says, you need to ask, *What does it mean?* These *interpretation questions* help you to discover the writer's basic message.

*Application questions* ask *What does it mean to me?* They challenge you to live out the Scripture's life-transforming message.

Fisherman studyguides provide spaces between questions for jotting down responses and related questions you would like to raise in the group. Each group member should have a copy of the studyguide and may take a turn in leading the group.

For consistency, Fisherman guides are written from the *New International Version.* But a group should feel free to use the NIV or any other accurate, modern translation of the Bible such as the *New Living Translation,* the *New Revised Standard Version,* the *New Jerusalem Bible,* or the *Good News Bible.* (Other paraphrases of the Bible may be referred to when additional help is needed.) Bible commentaries should not be brought to a Bible study because they tend to dampen discussion and keep people from thinking for themselves.

## SUGGESTIONS FOR GROUP LEADERS

**1.** Read and study the Bible passage thoroughly beforehand, grasping its themes and applying its teachings for yourself. Pray that the Holy Spirit will "guide you into truth" so that your leadership will guide others.

**2.** If the studyguide's questions ever seem ambiguous or unnatural to you, rephrase them, feeling free to add others that seem necessary to bring out the meaning of a verse.

**3.** Begin (and end) the study promptly. Start by asking someone to pray for God's help. Remember, the Holy Spirit is the teacher, not you!

**4.** Ask for volunteers to read the passages out loud.

**5.** As you ask the studyguide's questions in sequence, encourage everyone to participate in the discussion. If some are silent, ask,

"What do you think, Heather?" or "Dan, what can you add to that answer?" or suggest, "Let's have an answer from someone who hasn't spoken up yet."

**6.** If a question comes up that you can't answer, don't be afraid to admit that you're baffled! Assign the topic as a research project for someone to report on next week.

**7.** Keep the discussion moving and focused. Though tangents will inevitably be introduced, you can bring the discussion back to the topic at hand. Learn to pace the discussion so that you finish a study each session you meet.

**8.** Don't be afraid of silences; some questions take time to answer and some people need time to gather courage to speak. If silence persists, rephrase your question, but resist the temptation to answer it yourself.

**9.** If someone comes up with an answer that is clearly illogical or unbiblical, ask him or her for further clarification: "What verse suggests that to you?"

**10.** Discourage Bible-hopping and overuse of cross-references. Learn all you can from *this* passage, along with a few important references suggested in the studyguide.

**11.** Some questions are marked with a ♦. This indicates that further information is available in the Leader's Notes at the back of the guide.

**12.** For further information on getting a new Bible study group started and keeping it functioning effectively, read Gladys Hunt's *You Can Start a Bible Study Group* and *Pilgrims in Progress: Growing through Groups* by Jim and Carol Plueddemann.

## SUGGESTIONS FOR GROUP MEMBERS

**1.** Learn and apply the following ground rules for effective Bible study. (If new members join the group later, review these guidelines with the whole group.)

**2.** Remember that your goal is to learn all that you can *from the Bible passage being studied.* Let it speak for itself without using Bible commentaries or other Bible passages. There is more than enough in each assigned passage to keep your group productively occupied for one session. Sticking to the passage saves the group from insecurity and confusion.

**3.** Avoid the temptation to bring up those fascinating tangents that don't really grow out of the passage you are discussing. If the topic is of common interest, you can bring it up later in informal conversation following the study. Meanwhile, help each other stick to the subject!

**4.** Encourage each other to participate. People remember best what they discover and verbalize for themselves. Some people are naturally shier than others, or they may be afraid of making a mistake. If your discussion is free and friendly and you show real interest in what other group members think and feel, they will be more likely to speak up. Remember, the more people involved in a discussion, the richer it will be.

**5.** Guard yourself from answering too many questions or talking too much. Give others a chance to express themselves. If you are one who participates easily, discipline yourself by counting to ten before you open your mouth!

**6.** Make personal, honest applications and commit yourself to letting God's Word change you.

# SOMETHING AWESOME IS COMING!

Isaiah 65:17-25; Micah 4:1-5

*I wait for the LORD, my soul waits,*
   *and in his word I put my hope.*
Psalm 130:5

"When I build my dream house . . ." Many of us, dissatisfied with our surroundings or situation, have wished for something along those lines. Those who finally get the chance to build a dream house are often stymied. What *do* we want? What is really ideal?

Suppose you were building not the perfect house but the perfect world. What would you change? What elements would you leave in? What is missing from this present world that you'd like to see? God gives us a glimpse of a future remade world. What he chooses to tell us about it may surprise us.

♦ **1.** At the beginning of the 21st century, what reasons do people have to be hopeful? What reasons do people have *not* to be hopeful?

**Read Isaiah 65:17-19.**

♦ **2.** God promises to create a "new heavens and a new earth" (verse 17). At this point in Scripture, God does not yet describe them in detail. Instead, what do these verses emphasize about the new heavens and new earth?

♦ **3.** In the new creation, what experiences will God and his people share?

**4.** What words indicate that the joy of God and his people will be permanent?

♦ *Indicates further information in Leader's Notes*

**Read Isaiah 65:20-25.**

**5.** In the new creation, what sorrows will be missing?

**6.** How will the new world be more just and fair than the present world?

♦ **7.** In what ways does God the Creator promise to stay involved with his new creation?

**Read Micah 4:1-5.**

**8.** How does this passage establish the future prominence of the "mountain of the Lord's temple"?

14

**9.** In this future scenario, how will people show reverence to the Lord?

**10.** Describe the way relationships will change

between people:

between God and people:

**11.** Consider the coming new creation spoken of by both Isaiah and Micah. To what particular longings of your heart does it speak?

**12.** How do the images and language of these passages change or challenge your ideas about your hope for the future?

**13.** In what ways will the knowledge that this new world is coming make a practical difference for you today and in the coming week?

# A LIVING HOPE

1 Peter 1:1-9; Romans 5:1-5

*As the eyes of slaves look to the hand of their master,*
*as the eyes of a maid look to the hand of her mistress,*
*so our eyes look to the LORD our God,*
*till he shows us his mercy.*
Psalm 123:2

A deserted farm homestead, an unfinished basement filled with water, a wedding ring advertised for sale—all images that speak of dashed hopes. Look around at just about anyone's home and you'll see evidence of unfinished projects which have been abandoned. They were probably started with great enthusiasm, but they proved too difficult or tedious or expensive. The hope they brought for a while has died out.

In this decaying world, we all long for a *living* hope—one that transcends this world and won't fall into disrepair. And that is just what we have in Christ.

**1.** Who or what has recently disappointed you? Who or what has recently lived up to or exceeded your expectations?

18

**Read 1 Peter 1:1-9.**

♦ **2.** To whom is Peter writing and what is their plight (verses 1-2, 6)?

♦ **3.** Which thoughts in this passage are oriented toward the future?

Which thoughts are oriented toward the present?

**4.** According to Peter, how has the door to hope been opened for us (verses 3-5)?

♦ **5.** What is the relationship between future hope and current trials (verses 6-9)?

**6.** What is God's part in safeguarding our future?

**7.** In what areas of your own future do you especially need the assurance of God's safe-guarding?

---

**Read Romans 5:1-5.**

♦ **8.** What similarities do you see between this passage by Paul and the preceding passage by Peter?

**9.** What is the progression of growth that suffering can produce?

**10.** Based on both these Scripture passages, how does our hope in Christ give meaning to suffering?

♦ **11.** When have you found that your hope in the Lord has not disappointed you (verse 5)?

**12.** What are some areas of your life where the Lord's faithfulness in the past can give you hope for the future?

# HOPE FOR "SOMEDAY" = HELP FOR EVERY DAY

Colossians 1:1-23

*Even youths grow tired and weary,*
  *and young men stumble and fall;*
*but those who hope in the LORD*
  *will renew their strength.*
Isaiah 40:30-31

Suppose you knew you would inherit a fortune or become ruler of a monarchy at some indefinite future date. It might be nice to sit and think about, but what good would the knowledge do you now? You couldn't spend the money or issue any sovereign decrees. Life would be a perpetual waiting game.

The hope which Jesus offers is for an indefinite future time, but the Christian life is not a life of suspended animation. The hope of the gospel has solid results for our lives now.

**1.** How does waiting strengthen us?

---

**Read Colossians 1:1-14.**

♦ **2.** Why is Paul thankful for the Colossian Christians (verses 1-5)?

**3.** What are some of the results of hope which Paul sees in the lives of the Colossians (verses 4-8)?

**4.** Why do you think hope for the future has such positive results in the present?

♦ **5.** Consider how Paul is praying for the Colossians in verses 9-14. How do his prayers express confidence about their future?

♦ **6.** How do his prayers express confidence about the state of their lives now?

**7.** In verses 6 and 10, Paul uses the image of "bearing fruit." In verse 6 the gospel is bearing fruit all over the world; in verse 10 the Colossians' lives are bearing fruit. What are some practical results which are symbolized here by fruit-bearing?

**Read Colossians 1:15-23.**

**8.** What certainties about Christ does Paul express here?

**9.** How do you interpret the phrase "the hope held out in the gospel" (verse 23)?

**10.** How has the gospel given you confidence for the future?

**11.** Christ is described here as the One who is above everything and the ultimate reconciler of all things. These are cosmic-sized descriptions. What practical difference can these truths about Christ make in a believer's everyday life of faith?

**12.** In what areas of your faith would you like to be more "established and firm" (verse 23)?

# CONFIDENT IN HOPE

2 Corinthians 4:1-18

*May the God of hope fill you with all joy and peace as you trust in him, so that you may overflow with hope by the power of the Holy Spirit.*
Romans 15:13

When the famous Hyakutake and Hale-Bopp comets appeared in our night skies in the 1990s, some people took them as portents of millennial happenings. Now both are long gone on their journey around the sun. Meanwhile, things on earth continue much as they were before the comets came on the scene.

Whether it's a comet, a political impeachment, or an Olympiad, the most dramatic events slip into the past and out of the news, and life goes back to normal. Even "lifetime guarantees" have their fine-print limitations. We wonder, does anything have permanent life and value?

**1.** What are some things in our culture which seem dazzling for a while but which fade with time?

Scan 2 Corinthians 3. Then read 2 Corinthians 4:1-6.

♦ **2.** The word "Therefore" which begins this section refers to Paul's previous argument: that the "new covenant" of forgiveness in Christ is both splendid and permanent, and that we are being spiritually transformed as we continually turn to Christ. For Paul and his associates, what, then, were the results of these certainties?

♦ **3.** Paul makes a case for his honesty and his selflessness. Why would confidence in God produce these qualities?

**4.** This passage refers to "light" versus "veiling" and "darkness." In what way is light an appropriate symbol of hopefulness?

**Read 2 Corinthians 4:7-18.**

◆ **5.** After defending his own ministry, how does Paul now confess to his own failings?

**6.** With such a list of difficulties and weaknesses seen in verses 7-12, how could Paul still look forward with confidence?

**7.** Consider Paul's list of contrasts in verses 8-9 ("we are . . . but not . . ."). When have you experienced one or more of these (or something close to it)?

◆ **8.** What gave Paul confidence to speak out for Christ (verses 13-14)?

**9.** What will be the ultimate result of the gospel reaching more people (verse 14)?

**10.** How does Paul contrast his inward and outward state (verses 16-17)?

**11.** How does Paul's hope of eternal glory offer you encouragement in your everyday struggles?

**12.** This week how will you focus on what is unseen and eternal rather than on what is visible and temporary?

How can members of your group encourage one another to do this?

# LIVING OR DYING, WE BELONG TO GOD

1 Thessalonians 4:13–5:11

*Now faith is being sure of what we hope for and certain of what we do not see.*
Hebrews 11:1

A sure way to have a best-selling book is to write about a "near-death" experience. Many readers are eager to devour any firsthand description of what lies on the other side of death—even when it comes from a questionable source. Fearing the unknown, we hunger after any crumb of comforting information about the hereafter.

Despite all the popular books and discussions, we still know very little about life after death. We have not been there. But the Bible offers us a wonderful perspective on what we can know for sure.

**1.** What are some common ideas about life after death (or the absence of life after death)?

**Read 1 Thessalonians 4:13-18.**

**2.** What does Paul desire for the Thessalonian Christians who have seen death come to those they love?

**3.** We all have to deal with the reality that people we love will die. In the face of that fact, what are some differences mentioned here between those who have hope in Jesus and those who don't have that hope?

◆ **4.** Compare and contrast Jesus' future second coming with what you know of his first coming as a baby at Bethlehem.

**5.** When Christ returns, how will believers who are still alive be joined with those who have already died?

♦ **6.** Verse 15 indicates that Paul expected to be still living when Jesus returned. Obviously that didn't happen. How do you explain this apparent misunderstanding by the apostle?

**Read 1 Thessalonians 5:1-11.**

**7.** To what human experiences does Paul compare Jesus' coming (verses 2-3)?

**8.** Why are these appropriate comparisons? What light do they shed on this event?

**9.** For believers, what lessens the element of surprise concerning the second coming of Christ (verses 4-5)?

**10.** How should our anticipation of Christ's second coming affect our character now, while we wait (verses 8-11)?

♦ **11.** This passage encourages us to talk together about our certainty of Christ's return. Some Christians disagree and even exclude each other over the precise order of events before, during, and after Christ's return. According to this passage, what is a more appropriate reason to talk about Christ's return (verses 10-11)?

**12.** How does this passage affect your outlook on death—either someone else's or your own?

# WHAT CREATION LONGS FOR

Romans 8:18-39

*Rejoice that you participate in the sufferings of Christ,*
*so that you may be overjoyed when his glory is revealed.*
1 Peter 4:13

Frustration is never fun. We may see exactly what needs to be done, but we can't make it happen. Frustration makes us feel helpless and powerless. The cause may be a car that won't start, a relationship that won't be mended, a computer that keeps crashing, a rebellious person who won't listen to reason, or any of a hundred trivial or earth-shaking obstructions to the way we think things ought to be.

Paul takes the typical human experience of frustration and makes it global. The whole *creation,* he says, is frustrated! If that is true, it's even more remarkable that Paul expresses such profound hope.

1. In your opinion, what gives someone an undefeatable spirit?

**Read Romans 8:18-27.**

**2.** What are some of the present limitations of living in this physical world?

♦ **3.** Verses 19-20 speak of creation's "eager expectation" and its "frustration." How can both be true at once?

♦ **4.** How is the redemption of creation specifically linked to the redemption of God's children?

**5.** In what ways does the Holy Spirit help us in this "meantime" period?

**6.** What difference can this truth make in how you respond to daily frustrations?

---

**Read Romans 8:28-39.**

◆ **7.** What assurances does this passage offer:

about God's purposes for us?

about how God deals with our sins?

concerning God's love for us?

**8.** In what area(s) of life do you particularly need these assurances? Why?

**9.** How will this entire passage in Romans 8 affect how you pray about the future?

**10.** How will it affect how you pray about present circumstances?

**11.** Reviewing the passage, find all the reasons we have to live with hope.

# PROMISES KEPT

2 Peter 3:1-14

*"Yes, I am coming soon."*
Amen. Come, Lord Jesus.
Revelation 22:20

Standing in front of a happy couple about to be married, the minister said, "It's good to know that there are still people who believe that love can last and promises can be kept." A promise kept is a beautiful thing—especially these days when fulfilled promises are increasingly rare. We've lost our trust in advertising guarantees, smiling politicians, and sometimes even in the vows of marriage.

Jesus promised his followers that he would return to this earth. His hearers thought his return would be within their lifetimes. Now two millennia have gone by since that promise. Can we blame scoffers for asking "Where is he?" The apostle Peter reminds us that Jesus will keep his promise and shows why we can still live with hope.

**1.** How much thought do you give to the idea that Christ could return today?

---

**Read 2 Peter 3:1-14.**

**2.** What are Peter's purposes in writing this letter?

**3.** Why are "scoffers" so sarcastic about the prospects of the Lord's return?

**4.** How does Peter answer the scoffers (verses 5-7)?

♦ **5.** With what Old Testament events does Peter compare the second coming of Christ, and what are the similarities?

**6.** How would you paraphrase the statement "With the Lord a day is like a thousand years, and a thousand years are like a day" (verse 8)?

**7.** In what ways does this truth make you more hopeful?

**8.** Why does the Lord delay his coming (verse 9)?

♦ **9.** What will happen to the physical world at Christ's return?

**10.** How do you respond to this dramatic prophetic vision? Why?

◆ **11.** Knowing that Christ will return at an unknown future time, how should believers live (verses 11-14)?

◆ **12.** What makes this passage hopeful rather than frightening?

**13.** Think about areas of your life that need to be more holy and blameless, as you look forward to Christ's return. Pray together about these.

# HEAVEN—OUR HOPE FULFILLED

Revelation 21:1–22:6

*But we know that when he [Christ] appears, we shall be like him, for we shall see him as he is. Everyone who has this hope in him purifies himself, just as he is pure.*
1 John 3:2-3

Heaven. Angels strumming harps. . . . Streets made of gold. . . . St. Peter standing at the pearly gates holding a big key. Where do we get our ideas of heaven? Some images come from Scripture, certainly, but some come from fanciful artwork and even from cartoons!

No one on earth can say what heaven is really like. Many people have speculated about it, but the details are beyond our knowledge. More important than any detailed map or description is our own certainty that we will be there forever. Heaven is our ultimate hope.

**1.** What images and ideas does the word *heaven* raise for most people in our culture? For you personally?

**Read Revelation 21:1-8.**

♦ **2.** After his description of God's triumph in the last
great battle between good and evil in the book of Revelation, John records this final vision. What ultimate and
final transformations will take place?

**3.** Which words and phrases tell us that these transformations are forever?

**4.** What would it be like to live in a world like this?

How does this prospect give you hope?

◆ **5.** How does the Lord describe his future relationship with humanity (verses 2-4, 7)?

**Read Revelation 21:9-27.**

◆ **6.** How is the glory of the coming "new Jerusalem" portrayed?

**7.** What strikes you most about the descriptions given here? Why?

**8.** Why are no temple or light needed in this new Jerusalem?

**Read Revelation 22:1-6.**

**9.** How are images of nature used in this vision of heaven?

**10.** What will be the state of the Lamb's servants?

**11.** The Christian hope of heaven is sometimes ridiculed as "pie in the sky by and by," and Christians are accused of being "so heavenly minded they're no earthly good." Considering this entire portion of Revelation, how would you respond to such charges?

**12.** What effect does the hope of heaven have on your earthly life? What effect would you like it to have?

**13.** Take a few moments to look back through this entire study on "Ultimate Hope for Changing Times." How have these studies increased or deepened your hope in your future with God? How will you live more fully in that hope day by day?

# LEADER'S NOTES

■ **Study 1/Something Awesome Is Coming!**

**Question 1.** Some group members may answer in general terms of society, while others will take the question personally and talk about their own reasons for hope. The question has room for both general and personal responses.

**Question 2.** Although this is the message of God through the prophet Isaiah, it comes to us in human language which can never express the perfection of the new creation. The imagery conveys an ultimate reality which is beyond words. The passage emphasizes not the details of the new creation but the joy which it holds for God and for us.

**Question 3.** Notice how both people and God are described as rejoicing in the new creation (Is. 65:18-19).

**Question 7.** Note especially Isaiah 65:24. The Lord does not set up his perfect world and then leave it to run on its own. He promises to stay in communication with his world; and of course he will continue to rejoice in it (verse 19).

■ **Study 2/A Living Hope**

**Question 2.** "This letter is addressed . . . to Jewish Christians scattered throughout the world as a result of persecution of believers in and around Jerusalem. . . . The apostle Peter wrote this letter to encourage believers who would likely face trials and persecution under Emperor Nero. During most of the first century, Christians . . . could expect social and economic persecution from three main sources: the Romans, the Jews, and their own families" *(Life Application Bible,* p. 2256. Wheaton, Ill.: Tyndale House, 1991).

**Question 3.** Throughout this passage the language goes back and forth between what God has in store for us someday and the world we live in now by faith.

**Question 5.** The passage emphasizes that present trials are temporary while our coming joy will be forever. Trials now test and refine our faith, and they will increase our joy when Christ returns.

**Question 8.** Both passages express the fact that present troubles are preparing us for what is coming. Both acknowledge how God is bringing good out of trials. Both emphasize faith and joy. Both stress that these things are ours only through the new life offered through Jesus Christ.

**Questions 11 and 12.** While some group members may wish to keep their answers private, it will be good to encourage people to share if they are willing. We need to hear each other express confidence in the Lord; often we need to hear *ourselves* express it out loud to others!

## ◼ Study 3/Hope for "Someday" = Help for Every Day

**Questions 2 and 3.** Paul specifically mentions their faith and love which spring from the Colossians' hope (verses 3-4). It is good to stay aware that our faith and love are not simply private benefits, but they also encourage other believers and increase their thankfulness to God.

**Question 5.** Notice especially Paul's emphasis on their continuing growth and strengthening and how their lives would bear fruit and show endurance—qualities which are seen only over the "long haul."

**Question 6.** Notice Paul's obvious pleasure and pride in the spiritual maturity which the Colossians already have. His tone is one of satisfaction in them now as well as anticipation of their future.

## ◼ Study 4/Confident in Hope

**Question 2.** The results include not losing heart (2 Cor. 4:1), deciding to be forthright and honest (verse 2), promoting Christ and serving the Corinthian people rather than promoting and serving themselves (verse 5), having Christ shine in and through them (verse 6).

**Question 3.** Suggested responses: If we have confidence in God, we don't need to pretend about our motivations or play games with people, because our success isn't up to our own cleverness but is up to God. Confidence in God takes our minds off ourselves and our own wants, so we concentrate instead on what he wants and on the people he loves.

**Question 5.** Paul's honest admission of his own weaknesses is remarkable considering that he was also establishing his authority with the Corinthian church. His openness here is an example for all Christian leaders.

**Question 8.** While Paul had many reasons for confidence in Christ, he found strength in the certainty that he and the Corinthians would join in the resurrection of Christ (2 Corinthians 4:14).

## ■ Study 5/Living or Dying, We Belong to God

**Question 4.** Consider the infant Jesus' helplessness, his humble family origins, the "refugee" conditions of his birth far from home in emergency lodgings, the fact that few noticed his coming (see Luke 2). Contrast his second coming, when he will show his kingly power and everyone will see him. Both events have been predicted in prophesies and eagerly expected.

**Question 6.** First Thessalonians is probably the earliest of Paul's letters which we have in the New Testament. It is possible that at this early date, Paul expected Jesus to return soon. Later (for example, in 2 Timothy 4:6-8) we see an apostle who was reconciled with the fact that he was going to die. Another explanation is that Paul was simply expressing his identification with all believers, living or dead, including those who will be alive when Christ returns. In any case, Paul was not making an attempt to predict a date for Christ's return.

**Question 11.** Because we are sure Christ is coming back, we should "encourage one another and build each other up" (verse 11). We are going to "live together with him" (verse 10) so his coming should unite us, not divide us.

## ■ Study 6/What Creation Longs For

**Question 3.** Living in this world, before Christ's return, we live in a tension between what *is* and what *will be*. We know something tremendous is coming, but we also know daily that it isn't here yet in all its fullness.

**Question 4.** Notice Romans 8:19-20. It appears that when the first humans fell into sin, the creation in some way "fell" with them and is not the way God originally intended it to be. Our redemption will be accompanied by the redemption and re-making of creation, although the details of what that means are not made clear to us.

**Question 7.** Romans 8:28 is familiar to many Christians in an alternate translation: "And we know that all things work together for good to them that love God" (King James Version). Either way, the statement takes our faith out on a limb. But Paul was not pretending that all things, including sin, are good. "Romans 8:28 must be seen within the context of the redemptive purposes of God. In all things—in our suffering, groaning, hoping, waiting; in 'trouble or hardship or persecution or famine or nakedness or danger or sword' (Rom. 8:35)—in all things God is working 'for the good of those who love him.' That 'good' is the final and complete realization of God's love for creation, incarnated in Christ, from which nothing can separate us (Rom. 8:39)" (Manfred T. Brauch, in *Hard Sayings of the Bible,* p. 557. Downers Grove, Ill.: InterVarsity Press, 1996).

## ■ Study 7/Promises Kept

**Question 5.** In 1 Peter 4:5-6, Peter refers to the original creation (Genesis 1–2) and the flood, in which Noah and his family were spared (Genesis 6–9). You may wish to refer to Matthew 24:36-39, where Jesus himself compared his coming to the events in the time of Noah.

**Question 9.** The end of 1 Peter 4:10 may be read alternately that everything in the earth will be "laid bare" or "burned up." There is a clear picture of destruction in verses 10-12, but there is also a clear picture of re-creation in verse 13.

**Question 11.** The proper response to Christ's future coming is not to try to escape from a doomed society, but to "live holy and godly lives" in that society (verse 11). We should be pure, but not anxious; we should be at peace (verse 14).

**Question 12.** As a leader, it's good for you to stay aware that some group members may find this passage scary, especially if they are uncertain about their standing with Christ. Keep the discussion focused on the hope which believers have to hold onto. This session can provide a good opportunity to explain forgiveness in Christ and how being forgiven takes away our fear of judgment.

## ◼ Study 8/Heaven—Our Hope Fulfilled

**Question 2.** The "new heaven and new earth" recall Peter's description of our hope in Study 7 (2 Peter 3:13).

**Question 5.** The picture is one of intimacy on many levels: husband and wife, God living with us, his being not just God but *our* God, us belonging to him as his people, God doing something as tender as wiping tears from our eyes, etc.

**Question 6.** The immensity of the city and the beauty and costliness of its decoration are staggering. It is widely agreed that the city described is 1,500 miles wide, long, and high! The walls alone are 200 feet thick. Whatever else this description means, it certainly inspires awe, as does Ezekiel's vision of a future Jerusalen (Ezek. 40–48). The twelve stones of Revelation 21:19-20 recall the twelve stones on the breastplate of the Old Testament priest (Exod. 28:15-21), symbolizing the twelve tribes of Israel. The city is pure gold, and gold to this day remains the ultimate symbol of beauty and wealth.

# WHAT SHOULD WE STUDY NEXT?

To help your group answer that question, we've listed the Fisherman Guides by category so you can choose your next study.

## TOPICAL STUDIES

**Angels,** Wright
**Becoming Women of Purpose,** Barton
**Building Your House on the Lord,** Brestin
**The Creative Heart of God,** Goring
**Discipleship,** Reapsome
**Doing Justice, Showing Mercy,** Wright
**Encouraging Others,** Johnson
**The End Times,** Rusten
**Examining the Claims of Jesus,** Brestin
**Friendship,** Brestin
**The Fruit of the Spirit,** Briscoe
**Great Doctrines of the Bible,** Board
**Great Passages of the Bible,** Plueddemann
**Great Prayers of the Bible,** Plueddemann
**Growing Through Life's Challenges,** Reapsome
**Guidance & God's Will,** Stark
**Heart Renewal,** Goring
**Higher Ground,** Brestin
**Images of Redemption,** Van Reken

**Integrity,** Engstrom & Larson
**Lifestyle Priorities,** White
**Marriage,** Stevens
**Miracles,** Castleman
**One Body, One Spirit,** Larsen
**The Parables of Jesus,** Hunt
**Prayer,** Jones
**The Prophets,** Wright
**Proverbs & Parables,** Brestin
**Satisfying Work,** Stevens & Schoberg
**Senior Saints,** Reapsome
**Sermon on the Mount,** Hunt
**Spiritual Gifts,** Dockrey
**A Spiritual Legacy,** Christensen
**Spiritual Warfare,** Moreau
**The Ten Commandments,** Briscoe
**Ultimate Hope for Changing Times,** Larsen
**Who Is God?** Seemuth
**Who Is Jesus?** Van Reken
**Who Is the Holy Spirit?** Knuckles & Van Reken
**Wisdom for Today's Woman: Insights from Esther,** Smith
**Witnesses to All the World,** Plueddemann
**Women at Midlife,** Miley
**Worship,** Sibley

# BIBLE BOOK STUDIES

**Genesis**, Fromer & Keyes
**Exodus**, Larsen
**Job**, Klug
**Psalms**, Klug
**Proverbs: Wisdom That Works**, Wright
**Jeremiah**, Reapsome
**Jonah, Habakkuk, & Malachi**, Fromer & Keyes
**Matthew**, Sibley
**Mark**, Christensen
**Luke**, Keyes
**John: Living Word**, Kuniholm
**Acts 1-12**, Christensen
**Paul (Acts 13-28)**, Christiansen
**Romans: The Christian Story**, Reapsome
**1 Corinthians**, Hummel

**Strengthened to Serve (2 Corinthians)**, Plueddemann
**Galatians, Titus & Philemon**, Kuniholm
**Ephesians**, Baylis
**Philippians**, Klug
**Colossians**, Shaw
**Letters to the Thessalonians**, Fromer & Keyes
**Letters to Timothy**, Fromer & Keyes
**Hebrews**, Hunt
**James**, Christensen
**1 & 2 Peter, Jude**, Brestin
**How Should a Christian Live? (1, 2 & 3 John)**, Brestin
**Revelation**, Hunt

# BIBLE CHARACTER STUDIES

**David: Man after God's Own Heart**, Castleman
**Elijah**, Castleman
**Great People of the Bible**, Plueddemann
**King David: Trusting God for a Lifetime**, Castleman
**Men Like Us**, Heidebrecht & Scheuermann

**Moses**, Asimakoupoulos
**Paul (Acts 13-28)**, Christensen
**Women Like Us**, Barton
**Women Who Achieved for God**, Christensen
**Women Who Believed God**, Christensen

Printed in the United States
by Baker & Taylor Publisher Services